Before We Reached the Sea

Before We Reached the Sea

Poems by

Brendan McEntee

© 2025 Brendan McEntee. All rights reserved.
This material may not be reproduced in any form, published,
reprinted, recorded, performed, broadcast,
rewritten or redistributed without
the explicit permission of Brendan McEntee.
All such actions are strictly prohibited by law.

Cover design by Shay Culligan
Cover image by Guillaume Bleyer on Unsplash

ISBN: 978-1-63980-807-6

Kelsay Books
502 South 1040 East, A-119
American Fork, Utah 84003
Kelsaybooks.com

for Virginia

Acknowledgments

The Author is grateful to the editors of the following publications where these poems first appeared:

Blue Unicorn: "Carved," "Confetti"
Bloom: "There May Always Be the Trees"
First Literary Review—East: "Despise Nostalgia," "Retreat Wounded," "Cliffside II"
ink, sweat & tears: "Deathbed Wisdom"
Otherwise Engaged: "Dreamcatcher," "Grace at the Old Well," "The Fawn"
The Red Wheelbarrow 14: "The Great Wave," "Never Save a Drowning Man"
The Red Wheelbarrow 16: "The Children's Table"
Right Hand Pointing: "Before We Reached the Sea"

Contents

Confetti	12
Rave Ending	14
Despise Nostalgia	15
Clearer, Then Gone	16
Carved	17
Slouching from Sunshine	18
Retreat Wounded	19
What We Get	20
Inside the Rain	21
Feeding the Spider	22
The Children's Table	23
Dreamcatcher	24
A Defense of Small Truths	25
Cliffside I	26
Last Drive	27
A Last Act	28
Cliffside II	29
The Fawn	30
Spring Lamb	32
Swerve	33
A Quick Walk Across the Graveyard	34
Crows	35
Grace at the Old Well	36
The Holy Innocents	37
Smoke	39
Sentence	40
Lifelines	41
Wisdom and Silence	42
Resolution. Revelation. Catastrophe.	43
There May Always Be the Trees	44
The Last Castles of California	45
Cavities	46
Drinking in the Dark	47

Waterfall in Winter	48
None So Bright	49
Regrets for the Future	50
Drainpipe	52
Resigned to Ghosts	53
Before We Reached the Sea	55
Jetty	56
Whale in the River	57
The Great Wave	59
Under a Sky of Wet Metal	61
Boardwalk Traffic	62
Swimming	63
Dry Drownings	64

Confetti

In the midnight year
we were done
we were crushed
we fell like fresh rain
like confetti on the streets
absolved of living

Rave Ending

Four-on-the-floor and nothing's left but sweat and cadence.
Broken medicine bottles and paintings from Socialist Realism,
overdubbed with industrial gray, litter the floor.
Dread is the name of the song and we're dancing in this abandoned
　　factory.
Tomorrow, the same faces, scrubbed clean, will line up
For a new sermon, another carefully curated aesthetic.

Posters of kittens hang in the mold under imagined innovation.
A lifetime in miniature summed up on bumper-sticker grievances.
We whirl toward understanding—we sway toward silence, leaving

pastel blue for you, cadmium for me, and a doctrine
of misunderstandings colored outside the lines.

Despise Nostalgia

I live in pauses and edits. You lived fully, and so I'll never be able to tell your story the way it should be told. I'll never be able to tell her story, the sleeping woman in the pale green summer shift and white wrap falling off her shoulders, curled on a hotel divan, her ankles crossed, her rhinestone sandals revealing well-formed feet, just as her smile revealed well-formed teeth in an embarrassed grin when she realized she wasn't alone.

I'm lost to composition and excavation and can only tell how her smile became a concerned frown, how she knelt in front of a crying man in front of a sun-drunk room at the mountain's foot, much like the one where your remains would one day be cast, or how she hesitated, before wrapping him in tentative arms, offering soft sounds of comfort.

Clearer, Then Gone

The carousel's closed and will remain closed.
Behind the grate the animals fade; paint chips
from the tiger's eye, the peacock's feathers
blanche in the creeping sun.

The rain rivulets around my mouth and eyes.
There's no one coming to unleash the lions,
let loose the screaming horses or wake the sphinx
from battle-dream repose. No one's coming.

It's the old motifs I think of, stepping
through puddles and shaking the lift gate,
disturbing the trash gathered with rain-ravaged
leaves. Must and mildew— perfume

of the present. I imagine the calliope dirge,
the sound warped and tinny through bent speakers
wired to match the changing, charmed lights.
Then, I'd ride the basilisk with courage as the circle

came 'round, becoming mythic, a storybook hero
or something else, something other as my mother's
smiling face appeared and reappeared outside
the roundabout. Peering in; mortified,

sculpted faces appear, ghost-music sounds
hang on the early spring winds calling
back to when things were clearer, now gone.

Carved

Carved in the city,
Bedroom-birthed flower, precise
as x-rays. Smoke in the roses

and the spread of a parakeet wing.
This is purveyance
as sympathy. This is you,

willing: this is me
fumbling. No appropriate
maps. This is desire

for desire: too
long apart, hoping that skill
outspeeds the hunger.

The city crashes
outside. The hotel groans, sleeps.
I wake, hold my breath.

Slouching from Sunshine

There we were, a few thousand strong,
a milling congress of dogged expectation.
This was phenomena without us, standing giddy
in the moon's shadow, clicking away, careful
not to look up just as the experts warned us.

"This is what the eclipse was," we'd say,
showing photos of nothing, a dullard's day
photos that couldn't survive without
our explanation of the pull. But still

we hunted for transformation before the experience,
grinding it into another nothing. When it was over, the glow
fading faster than failed love, we slouched back down
the hillside, our shadows strong before of us.

Retreat Wounded

We made the best of a gray day, playing explorer
on a riverbank not far from the road. You hunted
heart-stones, ones that I'd fill in a bamboo bowl.
Bluegrass music floated down from a camp upriver,
reminding us that we weren't alone. You called to me,
and I went to you to look at the blood on the rocks.
Some attack, some fight, some animal survived
and retreated wounded into the forest. We followed
a ways, until I said that we should go back, concerned
about us, about you, to where we were wandering.
You wanted to press on, concerned about hurt,
wanting to repair. I won, letting nature take its course.
We returned to the car, returned to the hotel. I ordered
us wine and massages. Late that night, you spoke your truth
to the dark: "you should've let me help." Your stones,
sink-washed, dried on a towel in the bathroom.

What We Get

All these denying gestures:
how we cling to dead things
like a last leaf in a rainstorm.

How we seek out self-harm
striking with the sting of a tattoo needle
—forgetting the lesson
left with the mark.

Inside the Rain

In the closing roll of thunder, I look up from the sheltering
hotel carport. Your voice overrides the rain
and you wave, standing on the edge of the fountain.
The parking lot lights flicker as the dusk of a distant
hurricane tumbles over us. Cars sluice past, cutting
water into waves that wash over the curb.
Above us, flags twist like combatants,
snapping with unfelt ferocity.

Then I'm with you. We lock hands and look
into the water. Your laugh falls inside the rain.
Beneath us, backlit coins glow darkly in the waters
of the fountain. Burst with a love I imagine has
no limitation, I hold my thoughts and let loose
a quarter, watch it tumble into the fountain cascade,
disappear into the froth. A lightning strike, another
thunder warning and we howl in it, kiss for luck.

Feeding the Spider

In the back of childhood, in the contained summer damp
of the garage—our first storage solution—I brought

unwanted offerings to a spider. It was a thick, heavy thing,
the size of my thumbnail. It terrified me, confused me,

this creature living in our created space, to which I'd dreamed up
an unsolicited obligation. I pushed past grandma furniture

and abandoned toys: it would scurry to the corner of the window,
waiting for peace as I flipped last night's firefly or an ant

onto the strand of its lattice, waiting fruitlessly for it to eat.
It never did, not in front of me. Sometimes I'd watch

from the outside, peering through the shadows, study
the fragile spirals of its creation against the gloom.

Weeks—or years—later, I went to check:
found only an imprint of its web in the dust.

The Children's Table

Walking across the midnight fields banging pots and pans,
we were a scraggly army of children stumbling on uneven land.
    Ankles turned in divots, dust, kicked up by our heels coated
the backs of our legs. We followed her, our leader,
with trust and confusion. She was three years older
and always stuck at the children's table.
We marched and made noises against the passing

year. The rain erupted when we reached the spot the moon marked
for her. She uncovered the mistletoe in the plastic planter. We
reached into the earth, muddied now, and dug,
each hand put in for unity, though one of us kept time
 on an oatmeal pot, with a split wooden spoon.
We trundled home, stopping to paint the doorstops with mud.
She, being wise, passed through

the door with bread and stolen whiskey. We drank and ate.
We washed her legs and feet by the fire. We curled in bed,
we smelt her soap and listened to the devil-driven rain beat down.
"It's too late," she sighed and turned to sleep,
"the year's already lost." We stayed awake a
while longer, fingertips feeling her pulse beat blue
beneath her wrist, watching curtained lightning carve her face.

Dreamcatcher

The car smells of the living room and her stuffed animals. It was dark and Ada was sleepy when her mother buckled her into her car-seat. Now it was daybreak and light sprays through the window. She feels safe in sunlight. Ada watches streets she knows disappear, turn into highways, turn into the unfamiliar landscape of an unfamiliar country, traveling with her mother away from her father and house, his shouts, slaps, and silences.

The sun's warm and she touches the glass, surprised that it's cold, then touches her finger to her tongue to see what early spring tastes like. She breathes on the window, draws a cat, a heart, her parents, circles her reflection. Packed bags shift behind her. Her mother reaches back, touches her leg. A dreamcatcher with a crystal heart hangs from the rearview, catches the sun. Ada reaches through the spilling rainbow for her mother's hand.

A Defense of Small Truths

I walked, unweighted, into the ocean, allowing
sea water to fill my pockets, my eyes, and head.
I floundered by instinct, resisting before reason resumed
and I stayed still, sinking. It's likely I'll rise, body broken
on the rocks by the lighthouse, and I'll transform into random
trash, caught and strung in a tidal churn, a plastic bag
with passing history. None of this is fact but stands for truth.

And then there's you, somewhere before us, between sixteen
and twenty, standing in off-white capris by a bonfire, breathing
in the autumn cool from the inlet. You pull on the pill
of your sweatshirt, while pallets and shore wood scraps burn.
You sit on the edge of a chair, watch a new, fresh love
rough-house with friends while you tamp down your misgivings.
You'll always be hasty in romance, always turn away with regret.

You drain the molten rainbow flavors from your ice cup,
now the color of the bruises marking your forearm and side.
You're sugar-scorched as you press your tongue
to your sun-scored lips, rise and brush the sand from your legs
when you're called to play. You throw the waxed cup
into the fire, burn your doubts for a while.

Cliffside I

I was unfair in my expectation.
My father walked ahead of me on the narrow ridge, a footpath
carved on the sea cliff. We'd been here years before, a family
    intact,
and I'd walked this path, trailed a brother full of thought and
    prophecy,
who spoke to my sister and me on histories we knew
nothing about, trying to capture both meaning and moment.
I don't remember a thing he said to us. How could my father know,
his back facing me as we inched our way through headwinds past
    the safe
spaces, that I was reenacting that trip and the damage that
    followed,
turning grief over like the waves rolling below? When we paused
and he was about to speak and saw the tears of his youngest son,
pulled off and into the wind, his own face collapsed. We stood
in silence, our hands in our pockets, weeping alone in our losses.

Last Drive

Walking back to his vehicle from visiting the dead,
my father asks for the keys to his car.
I pause, but don't protest and hand them over.

Dignified as a hearse, he drives us
through the cemetery, pass weeping angels
and multiple mourning Marys

until we return to the aisle of our family.
He turns off the engine, nods his head,
slightly diminished in the seat. I don't say
"It's for the best" or anything

irritatingly aphoristic, just wait
until he opens the driver door,
leaving the keys in the ignition
and we change places.

A Last Act

Once the crowd drove off, the men moved in.
They were gentle, talking quietly amongst themselves,
pulling the green tarp off the dirt mound, getting the work done.
We'd stayed behind, small family, watching the internment.
Three bodies fit a grave: first a brother, then mother, now father.
It was late October, most of the trees were bare.
The wind held a sting, but the ground was still forgiving.
It's the last, firming act of adulthood when your parents die,
though I don't confuse it with maturity. I went to collect the girls
playing hide-and-seek among the graves; our footnote markers.

After dinner and recollections, I drove past the cemetery,
into the graying of late afternoon, looked for the grave
through the green gate. They'd set the flowers up nicely,
a momentary reminder for anyone who might pass by and see.

Cliffside II

We were foolish and giddy in our expectation. I knew nothing
of kites, but you'd wanted one, so I bought one.
A few weeks later, we drove up the mountain into the wind,
our unsuitable car creaking resentfully. Halfway up, a clearing
leading to a drop. We parked, you put up your hair.
It was hard for me to hold onto the starfish and spinner, but I got it
airborne, handed you the controls. You chuckled at the pull
and let it take you, running through the grass until
I caught you in a soft cross-tackle.
You'd come too close to the cliff's edge.
Were you only watching the sky?
The kite crashed and you scowled beneath me.
Days later, you glued squares of the kite's fabric onto the panes
of our French doors where it glowed greenly in our southern light.

The Fawn

for Kylie

The painted angels on the staircase are gone.
She doesn't remember them well
but remembers them well enough to miss them.
Everyone's in the kitchen talking, and she knows
they won't miss her, at least for a few minutes.
She goes through the door onto the sloping expanse,
wanders across to the crabapple trees. A thread
of cold rides the air as she picks an apple off the ground.

They startle each other, stare at each other.
She'd seen her just weeks ago when they'd been here
to say goodbyes. Then she'd kneeled in the window seat
beside the rented hospital bed and pointed her out.
He'd smiled and pointed as well, unable to speak
anymore, his eyes bright. Together, they watched
it wander in the thicket of trees by the barn;
there, then not.

It smells like nothing she knows: warmth
and wood and secrets. She reaches out, offers
up the apple, her souvenir now a gift. The fawn
steps back, then forward, flicking oversized ears
before snuffling her hand, velvet muzzle showing teeth,
taking the apple. Then she's alone beneath the trees,
and her mother is calling for her.

People head to their cars for the service.
She skip-runs up and toward the house,
fills her lungs to share. She thinks of the missing
angels and the feel of the fawn's breath on her hand.

Her mother puts her arm around her shoulders,
asks her where she went off to. She shrugs,
knowing it will suffice. She clambers into the car,
looks again for the fawn, knowing it will be gone.

Spring Lamb

It's a purchased slaughter, free-range and not FDA-approved.
A side business from his main milk and cheese,
which I bought at the Sunday farmer's market
in early spring. I took the idea home then we picked it out.
She knew what to look for, how old,
the breakdown she wanted.
But she didn't want to see it.

"You know, you don't have to be here for this," offers the
    sheepman,
"I know," I say. I'm paying though, and I want to see my part
    through.
We're in white overalls that smell of bleach
in a side room of the barn. There are rails with rope
and the floor gives way to a slope with a drain.
A stainless-steel table & a hardwood butcher block are off the side.

He brings the lamb into the room. Unsheared.
His son does a quick ankle wrap and truss.
Then it was in the air and the sheepman cut its throat
with a knife no larger than my father's pocketknife,
a fast deep cut across the two arteries, with intention.
He puts his hand on the animal positioning it over a trough,
holds it still. Less than a minute. It pulses blood, slows.
"He'll hang here for a while," he says, patting the lamb.
We'll get him dressed for you and I'll call you when he's ready."

I returned Tuesday with a large cooler. Three white moths
bounce around the daylilies outside the barn.

Swerve

At the top of the rise, I see it, a mile and a quarter down the road:
the deer, the car, the wrong swerve, the crash.

I pull up—New Jersey plates and a stunned driver
pulled off to the side, still holding the wheel.
I creep around the buck, about three years old, dead on the median.
I pull over, get out. August flies are already gathering in the blood.

New Jersey gets out as well. We check his car. Undriveable.
He's been up looking at vacation properties across the border
in Vermont. My green plates let him know that's where I live.
Not a native but seasoned. Always swerve in the direction
of the deer, I tell him, one dead buck too late. He feels bad
for the deer, for himself. "We've got to move it off the road,"
I say. He looks at me, nods. I take the hind legs, he takes the front,
stumbles over the head once or twice as we drag it into the brush,
the crimson smear turning black as we go. There's no cell service
and I offer him a ride to the service station a few miles down.

"I didn't see it," he says, trying to tamp down the apology.
"He was heavy," he adds after a minute. I try to reassure him:
"They can be tricky." We get to the town hub.
He's got bars on his phone and he stumbles through his wallet
for cash he doesn't have. "Hold on," he says, and exits to Stewarts.
I wait until he's inside before I drive away.

A Quick Walk Across the Graveyard

Five steps and I've covered two hundred fifty years.
Thin stones: granite, marble, and unintelligible.
New ones too, one dated within a few months.

A friend called me years ago walking through
a cemetery in Wales, filled with the dead of two millennia.
I listened to his amazement, his fathoming of time.

We're simply not so old. There are not so many layers of death.
Only the poets look back for lightning
and always too late. History is now and is
America. I'm a native son and this is not my soil.
Summer smells of moss and heat
left over from August fall through my hand.

At the package store across the road, I exchange "ayuhs"
with the counter-man. His family's there, he gestures with his chin.
One day he'll be buried there. Legacy.

In a diner, a couple learns infidelity
is disappointment and rot disguised as hope.
In a hospital, a couple looks at their newborn
and learns the terror of love.
I look at the collection of gravestones sighing *"please, remember,*
    please"
and pull into the trickle of traffic, eyes forward on the road.

Crows

The crows dot the field, taking in the morning
dew and sun. They're very present here.

They're on the roof of the antique center.
On the edge of the quarry.
They tok and caw and ruffle.

There's one tattooed on my chest,
above my heart. A guardian.
A blood apology.

The crows shift with the sunshine,
glistening like the dew as it burns.

Grace at the Old Well

She stands on the edge of the well's boards,
feels the creak before the sound, the shifting
of old wood. After a thought, she jumps back.
She'll tempt it again, testing her courage
for self-sabotage. Maybe tomorrow.

She walks across the sanatorium
to the algae-coated pond, her shadow
long beside her. The waterlilies have closed
for the day. They know something
that she doesn't
as the night bell rings.

The Holy Innocents

The children's ward is a place of tubes and crepe-soled shoes.
Cheery yellow walls, damaged by crash carts,
cartoon character appliques are torn at the edges
by small, bored hallway hands waiting for tests.
Calculated sunlight washes out rooms in this wing.

Children in wheelchairs call out,
setting times for board games
between bouts of medication and visiting
cadres of doctors on a learning curve.
Mylar balloons and cards are subtle currency.

Past the nurses' station are the quiet rooms
of PICU and NICU. Silence covers everything.
Charts and precautions dot the walls.
Equipment overwhelms the small bodies.

It's a simple procedure: disconnect.

She hears the doctor call the time.
She exhales, looks at her son
while despairdreadresignationresponsibility
pile together become their own car crash.
She kisses his bruised head between the screws.

She begins adjusting verbs:
"My son is." "My son was."
She watches his fingers turn blue
feels the cold of his leg

and the cold of the room.
She sees her ghost-reflection
in glass, her future face.

Smoke

The notes float down
from the store's sound system:
that love song, that break-up song,
that wedding song, all sung with smoke.

Keep your damnation. I've made this
inconsistency, this life of smoke
into something enduring:
the temporary falling into permanence.

Is this my reparation for living
beyond you, perfect in your wedding dress
and borrowed sweater, open casket,
while I, manikin, continue on?

Sentence

The last sparrow has left,
disappearing into the gray
of an oncoming thunder roll.

Where would repentance
go? If offered and rejected,
does it still exist?

I hold the sentence in my hands,
put it on—it's the only thing I own.
I smell the rain falling outside.

Lifelines

The man walks the line
of boxwoods marking the property.
He loses himself to sandbags
and bullets, sees them flow
out across the curving lawns.
A fox scuttles out and back
to safety in an oak tree.

Across the lines of his palm
crawls a searching caterpillar,
fallen from a tree. He stands
in an idle spring rain, holds
it out to an oak leaf,
and it regains its life's course.

Wisdom and Silence

I've sewn my lips closed
with the twin threads
of wisdom and silence.

Where silence lives is wisdom.
What wisdom leaves is silence.

Love is kept across the hall
infrequently visited, like an heirloom chest
of expectations, kept clean until opened.

Resolution. Revelation. Catastrophe.

Let's raise the old ideas from the bog and salt marshes,
share self-satisfied semiotics
with the unwilling pilgrims of the soft moments.
Let's maintain conventional insurrection
before we head to the basement, bars

and brownstones where we sleep and self-shame
and read poetry to each other.
Let's convert tropes to memes
in upended, colorful martini glasses.
Let's gloriously uncreate nature
and imagine we've overturned the narrative.

Let's call ourselves a victory.
Together, we'll untie the knot
and worry how we'll feel
if the sun does/not rise.

There May Always Be the Trees

Night came in early—November and a first
dusting. A cold stone wall, our dog, woods
beyond the field all becoming a mystery

at dusk. The fear of unnecessary injury
and the winding down of the clock
preoccupied me, though we didn't need

to be anywhere. I knew you were cold
but left you to your contentment, staring
into the space where the sun had fallen.

Our dog drifted into the shadows.
We could hear her light crashing
across the long grass of the fallow.

When headlights caught us, there
and gone, we walked back to the cabin
crunching across the gravel road.

I warmed the stew, and you went out
to the darkness of the deck, overlooking
another forest patch, allowing us to imagine

ourselves in an idyll. I brought you
a sherry and put my arm around your
shoulders. "There will always

be trees, won't there?" you asked. "There
may be," I lied. Inside, our dog whined.
We returned to candlelight and fire.

The Last Castles of California

We found a flower, a blue
lilac named "Dire Hope Breathing"
as we strolled the public gardens.

We drank wine over the smoke
of burning grapevines
in the last castles of California.

Cavities

It was morning but dusk flowed through us sitting on a sea wall
during our Northern tour with fresh coffee and egg sandwiches,
sea-spray misting our food, the sea foaming, bursting beneath us,
rising from the scarp. You rested your sandwich on top of your
    coffee.
Your restless hands pulled at the green glass cemented to the wall,
leaving your nails ragged with empty effort. A loose dog, a
    whippet,
ran in the lot behind us: you fed it half your sandwich and it licked
your bleeding cuticles. Its owner arrived and we spoke awhile.

"They call this the Witches' Cavity," he said with the awkward
pride of local lore. "They drowned girls here, you know, back then,
back when the weather got choppy and ships wouldn't come back.
Offerings, you might say. Responsibilities. Blame. Life for death
superstitions." We held that for an uncomfortable moment,
thinking of lives needlessly lost then chatted some more
above the storm-raged waters, what was happening,
what was coming, what weather always was, then gave
us a recommendation for the best blueberries in Maine.

You waved goodbye to Gordon, the dog, watched him retreat
across the way. I gathered up our trash, walked it to the wire can
half-expecting you'd be gone when I turned around,
relieved that you were still there. I stood behind you, wrapped my
arms around your shoulders, pressed my mouth to your crown,
felt your shiver, your arms wrapped around your abdomen, your
tears hot as they exploded on my wrist. I didn't say anything
neither did you—and we stayed in the warm, water-tossed air,
looking out to the violence of the sea.

Drinking in the Dark

Behind dead marriage walls I fill a shot glass with honey-tinged
whiskey and place it on a makeshift altar, devoted
to no divinity. I light a votive in a fifty-cent holder,
which will burn for the next few hours. I sit, try to pray, fail.

I remember our last trip together: you wanted to go
cliff-diving by the cross, hit the rocks below and live.
I slipped on the wet moss steps on the north side
of some cathedral, twisted my ankle, limped through.

I never think of home. We drive down to the canals
all the while having the old moral arguments, and I'm
secretly pleased that I never convince you.
It's been hours and the candle is liquid nothing.

Hours spent in fruitless rumination—is this prayer?
I lift the shot, toast your photo, and offer it to the air,
to the ghosts and gods that I know are not there,
as the votive gutters, drink it in the dark.

Waterfall in Winter

Slipping behind the cascade's curtain
which I imagine weeps for me,
I remove my shoes at the hollow's entrance,
shuffle to the candled corner,
replace the drooping lilies with fresh ones,
and cast the old ones into the crashing water.
But I've betrayed myself once again
and know I will never get it back.

Back on the ground, the air is shuffled
with the sound of thousands of Viceroy wings
in seeming contemplation of the river.
We imagined ourselves as waterfalls in winter.
It's hard to balance on these rocks and so I squat,
imperfectly capturing memory to overlay memory:
historical scrim. And I leave swearing,
as always, that I will never be back.

None So Bright

Weaving the garland through the bunting,
she promised she'd make it festive.
She stood in the snow-melting rain,
needling and cold, watched the lights glow
in descending gloom. Inside, evergreen
candles flickered by the tabletop tree
she'd picked up on the cheap.
A cardinal landed, shifted foot to foot,
shook and flew away at the sound
of an ice sheath falling into the river.
Then, only grayness, the glow of her lights,
and the rushing water remained.

Regrets for the Future

Deathbed Wisdom

The shadow of her arm falls long across the wall.
Once, she'd climbed a cypress in summer wearing an ivory shift.
Once, she'd kissed a stranger in a rainstorm who tasted of bourbon
    and sea spray.
The electric impulse of her stutters, fails.
Her body sighs.
The recording machines, always bright, always humming,
continue their work until they're switched off by well-trained
    hands.

Closing Chapters

He fled the hospital room just after she died
her post-mortem breath driving him out to the hall
full of weeping and noise. I followed to an empty
waiting room, his face a familiar composition—
an iceberg sloughing off into the ocean
without a swell of music covering the crash.
"What happens now?" he asked.
What I knew I couldn't tell him.

What I didn't know: that he'd be dead
in less than two years, the third siege of brain cancer
taking him from what could have been a grand
epilogue. He'd thought of selling the house, of traveling
with the kids for the holidays, shaking off the marital rigor mortis.

Instead, a casket and two ill-equipped twenty-somethings,
inhabiting their parent's home and carrying forward their parents'
regrets for the future, his cremains sifted into an urn next to their
mother, placed on the console by the flat-screen t.v.

Drainpipe

Unlike the irresistible river
clashing with the rocks, the spout
dripping on the bricks leading down
to my apartment offer no majesty,

though the eventual outcome is the same;
the water continues to carry and cut,
weathering out a victory.

The rain runs tracks down the frontier
of my face, strikes cooling drops
into my coffee mug as I watch
our dog mark out a new evacuation spot.

Business complete, I retreat to our cave
of aging and keep watch on time.
Above us, just level to my eyes,
the pipe continues dripping down.

Resigned to Ghosts

Being haunted is nothing special:
that bittersweet feeling of revelation without resolution.
It's in the amassed mess of a parent's estate, pecking out
the provenance of knickknacks, discovering amended recipes
in kitchen-stained cookbooks you never realized were read, or
reviewing youthful photos of your late spouse, living through
memories of vacations and love without you.

It's a child's death of Santa—realizing that holidays can still be
special but there were no guardians in the night except
for your parents about whom you're just understanding the divide
between their immortal love of you and their essential, flawed
humanity, a resentment you may never cross until, perhaps,

you have your own children, and you work through the night
carefully wrapping carefully chosen gifts, expended effort for
which you'll never get credit but that's okay because it's really
about love and those who passed before us, about whom you
wonder as you raise your glass of something, taking stock
of your life since they died, wondering if somewhere
they might be smiling, might be proud.
Because <u>you</u> are the magic they left behind,

keeping things afloat, carrying memory forward.
Being haunted is about endless resuscitation. Every special day
ends, falls over into one equally special and equally endured,
equally dull if you can't yourself create the illusion you require.
You can see it any weekday grocery visit to the frozen food aisle,
in the men shuffling with wrinkled khakis and worn orthotic shoes
they can't bother to replace. During the day it's the widowers,
picking through frozen dinners. Subsistence eating.

Subsistence living. At night, it's the broken and divorced men,
those suffering under the weight of their own punishments.

Those that renege haunt the bars, feckless failsons
drinking two-for-one beers, malfeasant and abdicating
responsibility. No matter.
It's there, the haunting, found in the slight turn
on the lower lip in the inevitable "Thank you" I offer
when the surprised apology occurs.
Sometimes, in sympathy, they gift you their pain,
to be folded up and stored with others.

Being haunted means that, despite desire, there's defeat,
pretending to write a different story without those
that you still hope are smiling somewhere, maybe nearby,
who you hope are thinking you're doing a good job at this living
thing or at least are forgiving because you yourself know
that you're not, and you know that loss
shouldn't be like a puzzle missing pieces
but a circle that breathes, that the inevitably of life
isn't supposed to be so anticipated or so resigned.

Before We Reached the Sea

An undershirt on a reaped corn stalk—
a wet tie stained with smoke—
water puddling in road scars.
The field, a former homestead—
the smell of burnt oil and skin fuse in the air
and soil, rising up even after the lavender blooms.

Jetty

The jetty,
like a bone spur
reaches out.

as waves cut
and drown the flowers
growing there.

Low tide dries
them, allows the spread
of new life.

Whale in the River

She lived as a coda, wore it like rain:
from her apartment near the overpasses
she could just make out the river.
She listened to the radio broadcast

from her apartment near the overpasses.
She watched the distant rescue attempt.
She listened to the radio broadcast
play out what she saw in her new binoculars.

She watched the distant rescue attempt.
Surprise became concern as the hours passed,
playing out in her new binoculars.
No one would say "doomed"

as surprise became concern. Hours passed.
No one would say "futile,"
no one would say "doomed"
but it hid behind their words.

No one would say "futile"
no one that knew her, not directly
but it hid behind their words.
Cloistered, she listened through the night.

No one that knew her, not directly,
would recognize her moving around her living room cathedral,
cloistered, she listened through the night
not wanting to gather, as many did, to coax and console.

Would anyone recognize her moving around her living room
    cathedral?
The binoculars brought a misplaced life into focus.
Not wanting to gather, as many did, to coax and console
this miserable, lost creature back to sea.

The binoculars brought a misplaced life into focus.
All efforts and tools: useless
in bringing this miserable, lost creature back to sea.
Overpass chatter broke on her like waves on the sea wall.

All efforts and tools—useless.
She lived as a coda, wore it like rain.
Overpass chatter broke on her like waves on the sea wall.
She could just make out the river.

The Great Wave

There's a woodblock of it at one of my favorite restaurants: striped mahogany and rock maple. My dinner companion asks the owner what it means. "That there can be no forgetting," he says, "to forget is to court reminding."

"Forget what?" she asks as a follow up question, her hibachi arriving at our table. "Forget that control is an illusion: we are in and of this world, not above it." He nods, satisfied with his answer, checks on other customers. She turns to me, confusion dancing in her eyebrows. I can see the skeleton in her and I regret at not having a more concrete explanation, so I drink my tea and redirect the conversation. We didn't last long after that.

She calls me two years later, leaves a message. It's late and her breathing is ragged. She tells me of her water dream, how she wakes up choking, imagining she's drowning. She's dreamt she's six and wandered from her parents blanket into the ocean. She slips on a sandbar and goes under a great wave,

tumbled and unable to find the sky. The current dumps her shore-side. She wakes and feels guilty, as if it were a failed ceremony, as if her destruction was a shared responsibility. Sometimes, on waking, she closes her eyes, looks back, feels her chest tighten at the relentless, thoughtless water beating on the shore. She thinks of the woodcut at that restaurant. "I want to see the wave," she says, "I want to know that I'm not answerable." She's acquired history.

She'd like to meet up, maybe for dinner sometime. She pauses, offers a soft goodbye before hanging up. I've never had a tsunami dream, and can't credit its symbolism and when I call her back, I'm sent to voicemail. I listen, I pause and hang up because I know that I'm not a lifeline, but an emergency buoy, marking wrecks.

Under a Sky of Wet Metal

Every day begins at five a.m.—the last hour
of promise in a pasteurized hotel room.

The one-cup coffee maker burbles
—I add powdered creamer into a travel cup

that I'll carry onto the shuttle but not before
I sit in a chair of bonded leather under a sky

of wet metal and whisper a half-hearted prayer
while looking across the landscape to the future

happening near the airport. Then I make the bed,
wipe down the countertops with tissues

pick up a glass, hold it to my mouth, mark it
with breath and put it back by the empty ice bucket.

Boardwalk Traffic

I'm watching the white line that is the ferry cling
to the horizon. Moving out from Port Jefferson, trailing
to an even thinner line, almost falling off the edge of the world.
New London is lost in haze. My finger, bookmarking a biography
on Raymond Carver begun four years ago and stalled,
grows numb, throbs under the weight of page and spine.
The ferry finally disappears. Loose sand blows like ash
thrown in the wind. A cloud, a gray finger, points the way north.

Swimming

Summer's heat has drawn down. All the lake house lights are dark
but yours. You sit on the deck's edge, your feet in the water
the copper glow of the kitchen light holds steady behind you.
while the moon's crescent is disrupted in the ripples.
Recklessly, you stand, shed your clothes,
slip into the lake and swim for the raft still out for the season.

You hoist yourself onto the raft and lay down. It's creak comforts.
You hum a burning song and push back your hair,
still heavy with the lake, and listen to the water pulsing
beneath you, heading down to the tributary, the river, the Atlantic.
Feeling sleepy, you slip back into the water, swim back
toward your waiting light, climb the ladder,
feel the milfoil slime on the rungs.

You sit outside the house, work a towel across your feet,
between your toes. Opening the slider, you step into the smell
of cedar. A late dragonfly bangs against the bay window
begging for access. You turn out the kitchen light,
look into the night. A rivulet of water
runs down your calf onto the oak planks
and you stay in an overly long moment, skin warming,
a lost hand resting on the edge of the sink.

Dry Drownings

We rush down to the wreck,
past the blossoming corpses,
and smash open the crates
taking what we can before
the alarms go up, before
the constabulary arrives.

There's a dream across the sea.
Cartographers scheme to keep it away
while the oceanographers name
angels in deep trenches far beyond us.
When questioned, we hold our silence;
we earthbound, ruptured submarines.

The unclaimed are laid across salvage boards,
covered with rushes and reeds: the flies
and crabs still come. At night, we gather
for the burning and sing the ocean song
where waves are as isolated as clouds,
where no one drowns alone in their own waters.

About the Author

Brendan McEntee is an alumnus of Hofstra University, where he acquired a master's degree in English Literature. He was a founding editor of *The Triggerfish Critical Review* and served on the reading board of *Now Culture*. His poetry has appeared in various anthologies and journals, in print and online. He is the author of the poetry collection *Servicing Nostalgia* (2019), and the chapbooks *manifests* (2017) and *Dimming the Stars* (2025). He can be found on Instagram at brendanmcentee.

www.ingramcontent.com/pod-product-compliance
Lightning Source LLC
Chambersburg PA
CBHW031204160426
43193CB00008B/501